D1709457

VOLUNTEERS:
MAKING
OUR COUNTRY
BETTER

By Charlotte Taylor

DISCOVER!

Enslow
PUBLISHING

Please visit our website, www.enslow.com. For a free color catalog of all our high-quality books, call toll free 1-800-398-2504 or fax 1-877-980-4454.

Library of Congress Cataloging-in-Publication Data

Library of Congress Cataloging-in-Publication Data
Names: Taylor, Charlotte, 1978- author.
Title: Volunteers : making our country better / Charlotte Taylor.
Description: New York : Enslow Publishing, [2021] | Series: Being a U.S.
   citizen | Includes bibliographical references and index. | Contents:
   Words to Know – Let's All Help! – People Helping People – Furry
   Friends in Need – Fresh Air Volunteers – Cash for a Cause – Get
   Started – For More Information – Index.
Identifiers: LCCN 2019050649 | ISBN 9781978517608 (library binding) | ISBN
   9781978517622 (paperback) | ISBN 9781978517592 | ISBN 9781978517615
   (ebook)
Subjects: LCSH: Voluntarism–United States–Juvenile literature. |
   Voluntarism–Juvenile literature.
Classification: LCC HN90.V64 T39 2021 | DDC 302/.14–dc23
LC record available at https://lccn.loc.gov/2019050649

Published in 2021 by
Enslow Publishing
101 West 23rd Street, Suite #240
New York, NY 10011

Designer: Laura Bowen
Editor: Megan Quick

Photo credits: Cover, pp. 1, 10, 20 (hands, hearts) Tetiana Yurchenko/Shutterstock.com; pp. 4, 12 ann131313/Shutterstock.com; p. 5 fstop123/E+/Getty Images; p. 6 Dmitry Natashin/Shutterstock.com; p. 7 monkeybusinessimages/iStock.com; p. 8 Sararoom Design/ Shutterstock.com; p. 9 SeventyFour/iStock.com; pp. 11, 21 SDI Productions/E+/Getty Images; p. 13 FatCamera/iStock/Getty Images Plus/ Getty Images; p. 14 JoseDLF/Wikimedia Commons; p. 15 hedgehog94/Shutterstock.com; p. 16 MicroOne/Shutterstock.com; p. 17 SDI Productions/iStock/Getty Images Plus/Getty Images; p. 18 Quarta/Shutterstock.com; p. 19 Monkey Business Images/ Shutterstock.com.

Portions of this work were originally authored by Richard Pickman and published as *Let's Volunteer!* All new material in this edition was authored by Charlotte Taylor.

Printed in the United States of America

Some of the images in this book illustrate individuals who are models. The depictions do not imply actual situations or events.

CPSIA compliance information: Batch #BS20ENS: For further information contact Enslow Publishing, New York, New York, at 1-800-398-2504.

Find us on

CONTENTS

Boldface words appear in Words to Know.

LET'S ALL HELP!

We are all part of a **community**. It is important to help your community. One way to help is to be a volunteer. A volunteer is a person who works without being paid. A volunteer helps others. There are many ways to volunteer. You can help people, animals, or Earth.

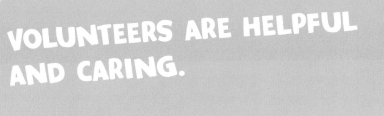
VOLUNTEERS ARE HELPFUL AND CARING.

Donations

5

PEOPLE HELPING PEOPLE

If you have older people who live near you, ask if they need help. You can do jobs around the house or in the yard. You can shovel snow for them. You can cook or do a craft together. Or you can sit and talk to each other.

TAKE SOME TIME TO TALK WITH AN OLDER NEIGHBOR.

You can also help people who are sick. You can make cards for people who are in the **hospital**. Cards help **cheer** up people who are sick. They are fun to make too. It feels good to make other people happy.

A CARD MEANS A LOT TO SOMEONE WHO IS SICK.

9

Another way to help people is to volunteer at a soup kitchen. This is a place where people go if they don't have money for food. They get free food at the soup kitchen. It is an important place in the community.

YOUR WHOLE FAMILY CAN HELP OUT AT A SOUP KITCHEN.

FURRY FRIENDS IN NEED

Animals need your help! You can volunteer at an animal **shelter**. The animals there don't have homes. They need people to care for them. You can walk dogs or play with cats. You may also feed the animals or clean cages.

MANY SHELTER ANIMALS NEED SOMEONE TO PLAY WITH.

13

FRESH AIR VOLUNTEERS

There are lots of places to volunteer outdoors. Do you have a park in your neighborhood? Get a group of friends together. Clean up the park by picking up trash and throwing it away or **recycling**. You can help keep your community beautiful!

CLEANING UP A PARK IS FUN
WHEN YOU DO IT WITH A FRIEND.

You can help Earth by planting flowers or trees. Some volunteers plant trees in parks. Others work in a community garden. Start with some seeds and watch them grow! If there is no community garden where you live, start your own.

PLANTING TREES IS GOOD FOR EARTH.

CASH FOR A CAUSE

A great way to volunteer is to hold a **fundraiser**. The money you make goes to people in need. You can help out at a car wash or make cookies for a bake sale. Fundraisers are fun and helpful.

A BAKE SALE IS A YUMMY WAY TO RAISE MONEY!

19

GET STARTED

Volunteers do a lot of good. They also have fun, meet new people, and learn new things. So, find someone who needs help. Talk to your neighbors, check with your school or church, or visit places in town. It feels good to help!

WHEN YOU VOLUNTEER, YOU MAKE YOUR COMMUNITY A BETTER PLACE.

WORDS TO KNOW

cheer To make happy.

community A group of people living in a certain place.

fundraiser An event that is held to raise money.

hospital A place where sick or hurt people are given care.

recycle To treat something so it can be used again instead of throwing it away.

shelter A place where animals or people are kept safe.

FOR MORE INFORMATION

Books

Higginson, Sheila Sweeny. *Kids Who Are Changing the World*. New York, NY: Simon Spotlight, 2019.

McCloud, Carol. *Bucket Filling from A to Z*. Brighton, MI: Bucket Fillers, 2017.

Websites

Be a Volunteer
kidshealth.org/en/kids/volunteering.html
Check out lots of ideas for how and where to volunteer.

Kids That Do Good
kidsthatdogood.com
Learn more about volunteering and the groups you can help.

INDEX